IRA PITTELMAN   TOM HULCE   JEFFREY RICHARDS   JERRY FRANKEL

ATLANTIC THEATER COMPANY

Jeffrey Sine   Freddy DeMann   Max Cooper

Mort Swinsky/Cindy and Jay Gutterman/Joe McGinnis/Judith Ann Abrams
ZenDog Productions/CarJac Productions
Aron Bergson Productions/Jennifer Manocherian/Ted Snowdon
Harold Thau/Terry Schnuck/Cold Spring Productions
Amanda Dubois/Elizabeth Eynon Wetherell
Jennifer Maloney/Tamara Tunie/Joe Cilibrasi/StyleFour Productions

present

Book & Lyrics by
Steven Sater

Music by
Duncan Sheik

Based on the play by
Frank Wedekind

with

Skylar Astin   Gerard Canonico   Lilli Cooper   Jennifer Damiano   Rob Devaney
Christine Estabrook   John Gallagher, Jr.   Gideon Glick   Jonathan Groff   Robert Hager
Brian Charles Johnson   Frances Mercanti-Anthony   Lea Michele   Lauren Pritchard   Krysta Rodriguez
Stephen Spinella   Phoebe Strole   Jonathan B. Wright   Remy Zaken

Scenic Design	Costume Design	Lighting Design	Sound Design
Christine Jones	**Susan Hilferty**	**Kevin Adams**	**Brian Ronan**

Orchestrations	Vocal Arrangements	Additional Arrangements	Music Coordinator
Duncan Sheik	**AnnMarie Milazzo**	**Simon Hale**	**Michael Keller**

Casting	Fight Direction	Production Stage Manager	Associate Producers
Jim Carnahan, C.S.A. **Carrie Gardner**	**J. David Brimmer**	**Heather Cousens**	**Joan Cullman Productions** **Patricia Flicker Addiss**

Technical Supervision	General Management	Press Representative
Neil A. Mazzella	**Abbie M. Strassler**	**Jeffrey Richards Associates**

Music Director
Kimberly Grigsby

Choreography
Bill T. Jones

Directed by
Michael Mayer

Originally produced by the Atlantic Theater Company by special arrangement with Tom Hulce & Ira Pittelman.
The producers wish to express their appreciation to the Theatre Development Fund for its support of this production.

Cover photo: Monique Carboni
Cover art courtesy of Serino Coyne, Inc.
All arrangements by Duncan Sheik
Special thanks to Deborah Abramson for her noteworthy contributions

ISBN 13: 978-1-4234-3133-6

HAL•LEONARD®
CORPORATION

7777 W. BLUEMOUND RD. P.O. BOX 13819 MILWAUKEE, WI 53213

Visit Hal Leonard Online at
www.halleonard.com

Jonathan Groff & Lea Michele
© Monique Carboni

Christine Estabrook
© Joan Marcus

John Gallagher,
© Doug Hami

an Groff, Skylar Astin, John Gallagher, Jr. & Company
Marcus

Jonathan Groff & Stephen Spinella
© Joan Marcus

John Gallagher, Jr., Jonathan B. Wright, Skylar Astin & Gideon Glick
© Joan Marcus

Jonathan Groff
© Joan Marcus

Jonathan Groff & John Gallagher, Jr.
© Joan Marcus

Remy Zaken, Phoebe Strole,
Lea Michele & Lilli Cooper
© Joan Marcus

Lea Michele & Jonathan Groff
© Joan Marcus

Lauren Pritchard
© Joan Marcus

John Gallagher, Jr. & Stephen Spinella
© Joan Marcus

CONTENTS

Steven Sater & Duncan Sheik

© Monique Carboni

MAMA WHO BORE ME

Music by DUNCAN SHEIK
Lyrics by STEVEN SATER

ALL THAT'S KNOWN

Music by DUNCAN SHEIK
Lyrics by STEVEN SATER

Hypnotically, at a moderate tempo

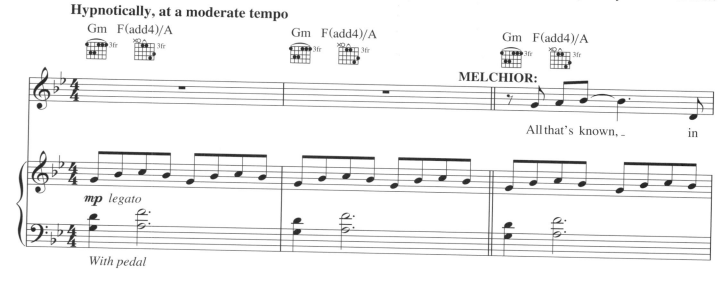

MELCHIOR:

All that's known, in

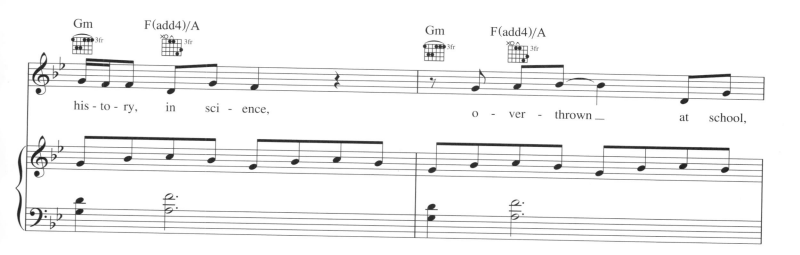

his-to-ry, in sci-ence, o-ver-thrown at school,

at home, by blind men. You doubt them, and soon they bark and hound you 'til

THE BITCH OF LIVING

Music by DUNCAN SHEIK
Lyrics by STEVEN SATER

out, out of this night - mare." Then I heard her sil - ver call. ___ She

said, "Just give it time, ___ kid. I come to one and all." She said,

OTHER BOYS:

Ah. ___

"Give me that hand, please, and the itch you can't con - trol. Let me

Ah. ___

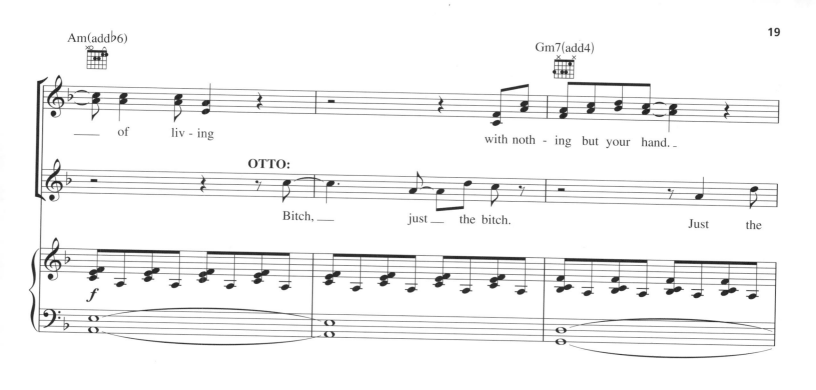

of liv-ing with noth-ing but your hand.

OTTO: Bitch, ___ just ___ the bitch. Just the

Just the bitch ___ of liv-ing as some-one you can't stand. ___

GEORG: See, each

bitch, yeah. Just the bitch ___ of liv-ing as some-one you can't stand. ___

night, it's, like, fan-tas-tic toss-ing, turn-ing, with-out rest, 'cause my day's at the pi-an-o with my

Gm7(add4)   B♭sus2

ERNST:

Oh, __ who knows? _____

See, there's

OTHER BOYS:

Ah. _____

dim.

Fmaj7(add4)   **HANSCHEN:**   F7(add4)

show-er-ing __ in gym class...   Bob-by Ma-ler, he's the best... __

Ah. _____

mp

B♭maj7/F   **ERNST:**

Looks so nas-ty in those __ khak-is... _____

God, my

Ah. _____   Ah. _____

B♭sus2

MELCHIOR:

ALL:

Just the bitch ___ of liv - ing and know - ing this is it. ___ God, is ___

Am(add♭6)

Gm7(add4)

___ this it? ___ This can't _ be it. ___

B♭sus2

F

Oh, God, what a bitch!

MY JUNK

Music by DUNCAN SHEIK
Lyrics by STEVEN SATER

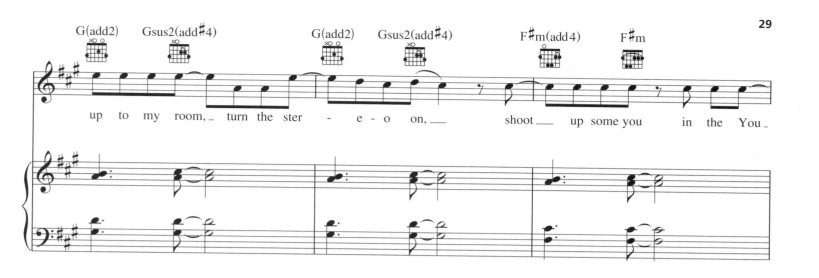

up to my room,__ turn the ster - e - o on,__ shoot__ up some you in the You_

THEA:

___ of some song. I lie__ back, just drift - in', and play__ out these scenes.__ I

ALL OTHERS:

I lie back, drift - in', these scenes,_

ANNA:

ride on the rush,_ all the hopes,_ all the dreams.__ I may__ be ne - glect - in' the things_

the rush, the__ dreams.__

TOUCH ME

Music by DUNCAN SHEIK
Lyrics by STEVEN SATER

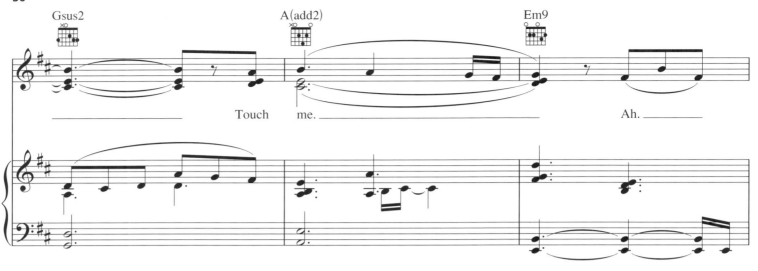

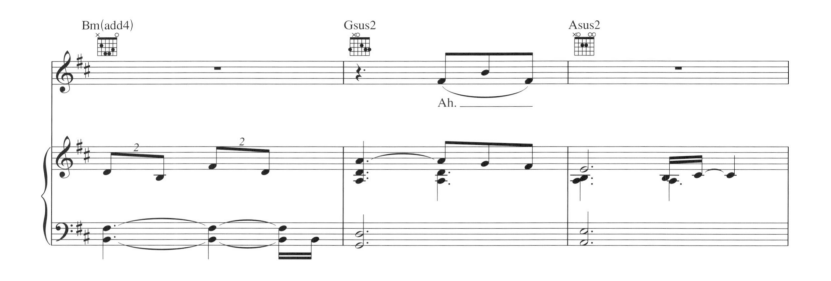

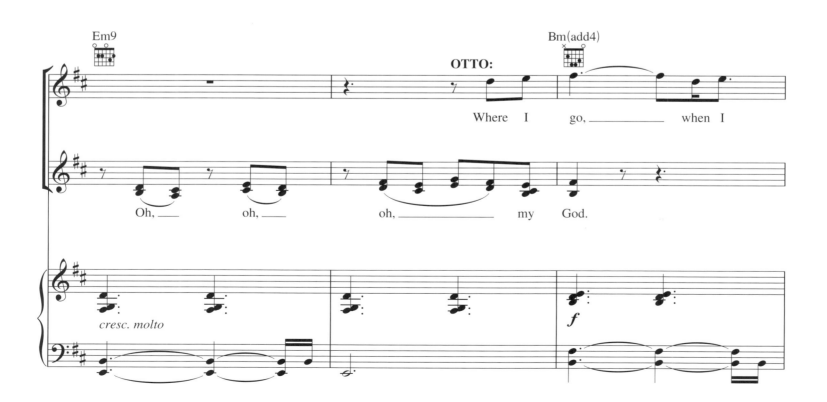

Girls match Boys' register, one octave below written.

THE WORD OF YOUR BODY

Music by DUNCAN SHEIK
Lyrics by STEVEN SATER

THE DARK I KNOW WELL

Music by DUNCAN SHEIK
Lyrics by STEVEN SATER

Moderately fast, with intensity

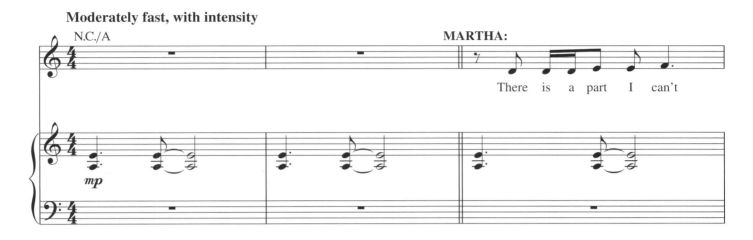

There is a part I can't

tell   'bout the dark __ I know __ well. _____

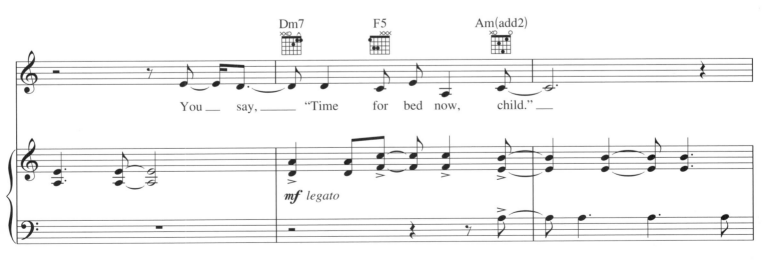

You __ say, _____ "Time   for bed now,   child." __

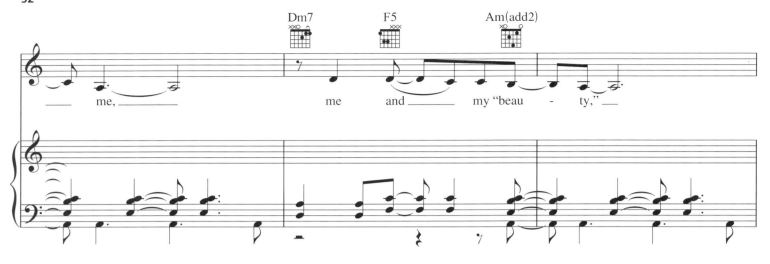

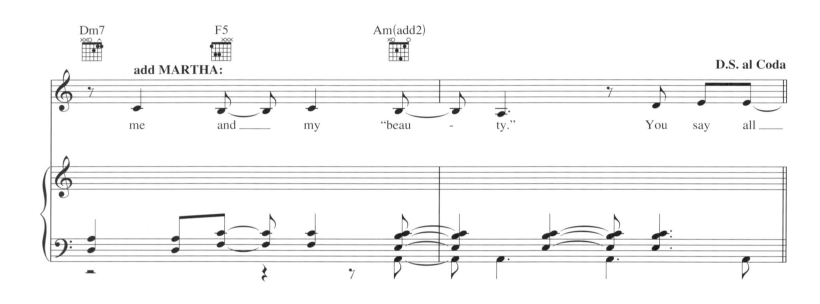

AND THEN THERE WERE NONE

Music by DUNCAN SHEIK
Lyrics by STEVEN SATER

THE MIRROR-BLUE NIGHT

Music by DUNCAN SHEIK
Lyrics by STEVEN SATER

out of peace with no keys to my soul.

BOYS:

And the whis - pers of fear, the chill

I BELIEVE

Music by DUNCAN SHEIK
Lyrics by STEVEN SATER

I be-lieve. ___

I be-lieve. ___

All ___ will be ___ for-giv-en.

There is love ___ in Heav - en. ___

I be-lieve. ___

I be-lieve. ___

All ___ will be ___ for-giv-en.

There is love ___ in Heav - en. ___

DON'T DO SADNESS/BLUE WIND

Music by DUNCAN SHEIK
Lyrics by STEVEN SATER

Play cues 2nd time only.

THE GUILTY ONES

Music by DUNCAN SHEIK
Lyrics by STEVEN SATER

Some-thing's started cra-zy, sweet and un-known.

Some-thing you keep in a box on the street,

LEFT BEHIND

Music by DUNCAN SHEIK
Lyrics by STEVEN SATER

Freely, slowly

Steady tempo, gently

MELCHIOR:

You fold his hands and smooth his tie, ___ you gen-tly lift his chin. ___ Were you real-ly so blind and un-kind ___ to him? Can't help the itch to touch, to kiss, to

Girls match Boys' register, one octave below written.

Girls match Boys' register, one octave below written.

Girls sing at pitch.

*Girls sing at pitch.

C(add2)   F6/9   Am11   C(add2)   F6/9

add GIRLS:*

oh. _____   A

G7(no3)   C/G   Cm/G   G   Cm6/G   G   C/G   G

shad - ow passed, _ a shad - ow passed, _ yearn - ing, yearn - ing

A7   Cmaj9

for   the   fool   it   called   a   home. _____

Csus2

MELCHIOR:

And it

Girls match Boys' register, one octave below written.

*All Girls and Boys sing at pitch.

TOTALLY FUCKED

Music by DUNCAN SHEIK
Lyrics by STEVEN SATER

Moderately fast Rock

MELCHIOR: There's a mo-ment you know _ you're fucked.

Not an inch ___ more room _ to self-de-struct. ___ No more moves, _

Girls match Boys' register, one octave below written.

Girls match Boys' register, one octave below written.

*Boys sound one octave lower; Girls as written.

WHISPERING

Music by DUNCAN SHEIK
Lyrics by STEVEN SATER

THOSE YOU'VE KNOWN

Music by DUNCAN SHEIK
Lyrics by STEVEN SATER

world grows dark a - round __ you and noth-ing is the same __ un - til you

know that they have found __ you. _____

Moderately

mp legato, with a beat

WENDLA: Those you've pained __ may

car - ry that __ still with them... all the same, __ they

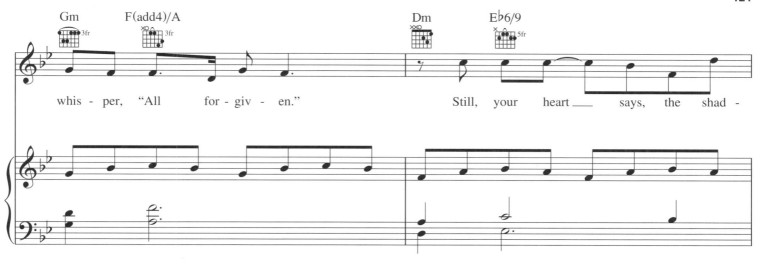

whis - per, "All for - giv - en." Still, your heart ___ says, the shad -

ows bring the star light and ev-'ry-thing you've ev - er been is still ___

___ there in the dark ___ night. ___ When the north - ern wind ___ blows, the

MORITZ:

Though you know ___ you've left them far be - hind, ___ you

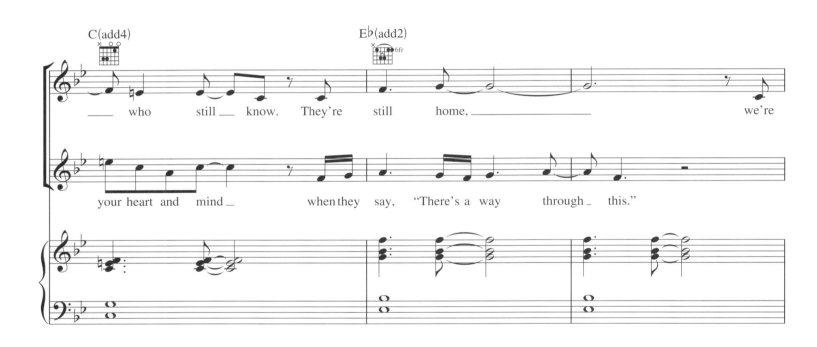

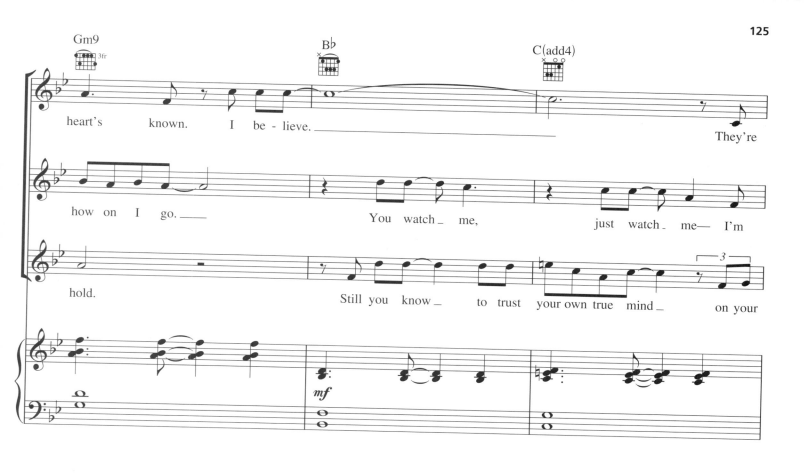

THE SONG OF PURPLE SUMMER

Music by DUNCAN SHEIK
Lyrics by STEVEN SATER

Slow, a little freely at first

ILSE:
Lis-ten to what's in the heart of a child: _ a

song so big _ in one _ so small. _ Soon you will hear where beau - ty lies. You'll

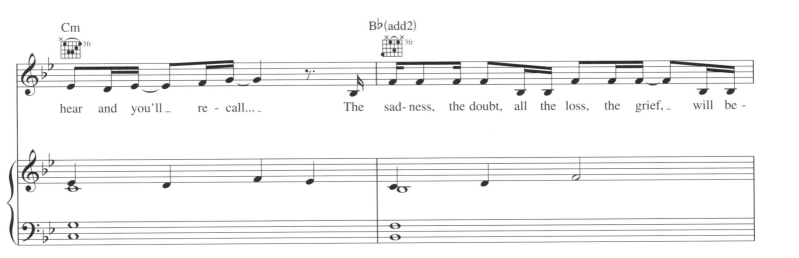

hear and you'll _ re - call.... The sad-ness, the doubt, all the loss, the grief, _ will be-

*All sing at pitch.
**Male voices (upper notes) sound one octave lower.

*Male voices (upper notes) sound one octave lower.

*All shown at pitch this staff.

I will sing the song of pur-ple sum-mer.

I will sing the song of pur-ple sum-mer.

All shall know the won - der of pur - ple sum -

All shall know the won - der of pur - ple sum -

mer.

mer.